Looking at Maps

Understanding Grid Co...

Moira Anderson

Publishing Credits

Editor
Sara Johnson

Editorial Director
Emily R. Smith, M.A.Ed.

Editor-in-Chief
Sharon Coan, M.S.Ed.

Creative Director
Lee Aucoin

Publisher
Rachelle Cracchiolo, M.S.Ed.

Image Credits

The author and publisher would like to gratefully credit or acknowledge the following for permission to reproduce copyright material: cover, Alamy; p.1, Istock Photo; p.4, U.S. Geological Survey; p.4, (inset) NOAA; p.5, Lonely Planet Images; p.7, Istock Photo; p.8, Country Cartographics, Victoria; p.13, Shutterstock; p.16, The Photolibrary; p.18, Istock Photo; p. 20, Lonely Planet Images; p.21, U.S. Geological Survey; p.22, Shutterstock; p.23, Country Cartographics, Victoria; p.24, Alamy; p.25, Istock Photo; p.25, (inset) Newspix; p.26, U.S Library of Congress. Illustrations on pp. 6, 10, 11, 14, 15, 17, 19, 27, and 28 by Lewis Chandler.

While every care has been taken to trace and acknowledge copyright, the publishers tender their apologies for any accidental infringement where copyright has proved untraceable. They would be pleased to come to a suitable arrangement with the rightful owner in each case.

Teacher Created Materials

5301 Oceanus Drive
Huntington Beach, CA 92649-1030
http://www.tcmpub.com
ISBN 978-0-7439-0899-3
© 2009 Teacher Created Materials Publishing

Table of Contents

What Are Maps?

Maps are special pictures that give information. Maps can show us where things are. They can also show us how to get somewhere. And maps can show us how far away a place is.

▼ **This road map shows part of the United States.**

Weather Maps

Weather maps are used to **forecast** the weather.

A map is a detailed **image** of an area. A map shows what the area looks like from above.

Often, a map shows a large area as a small picture. The streets in a city can be shown on a street map like this.

▼ **A street map of Sydney, Australia**

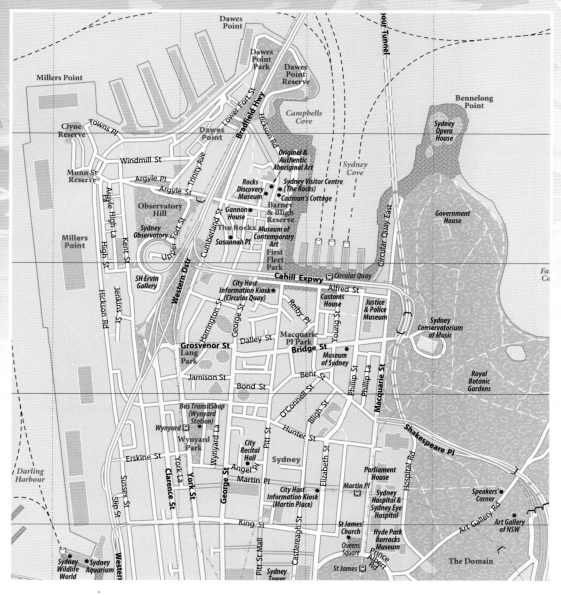

Grid Coordinates

A map can show us the **locations** (lo-KAY-shuhns) of things and places. A grid of lines is put over a map. The grid lines form cells. Each cell has a letter and number. These are called grid coordinates. In the map below, cell A1 is shaded blue.

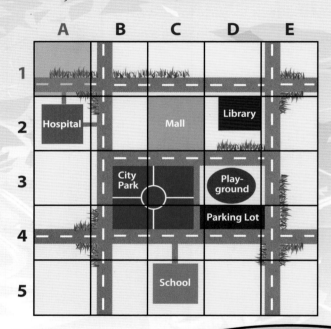

LET'S EXPLORE MATH

Look at the street map above. Write the grid coordinates for these places:

a. mall   **c.** playground   **e.** hospital

b. library   **d.** parking lot   **f.** school

Longitude and Latitude

Some maps of Earth have vertical and horizontal grid lines. The vertical lines are known as **longitude** (LAHN-juh-tood). The horizontal lines are known as **latitude** (LAT-uh-tood). The coordinates of these grid lines give the locations of different parts of the world.

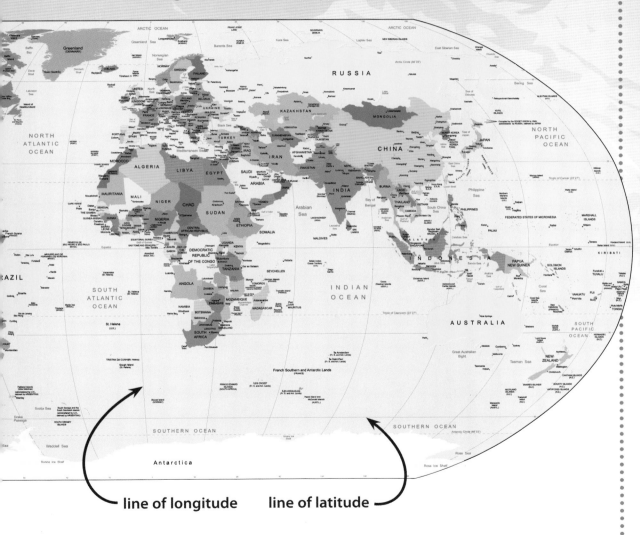

line of longitude   line of latitude

Atlases

An atlas is a book of maps. Some atlases also have charts and tables. Most atlases have photographs, too. The maps may show countries and cities. They may also show **features** (FEE-churz) such as mountains and rivers.

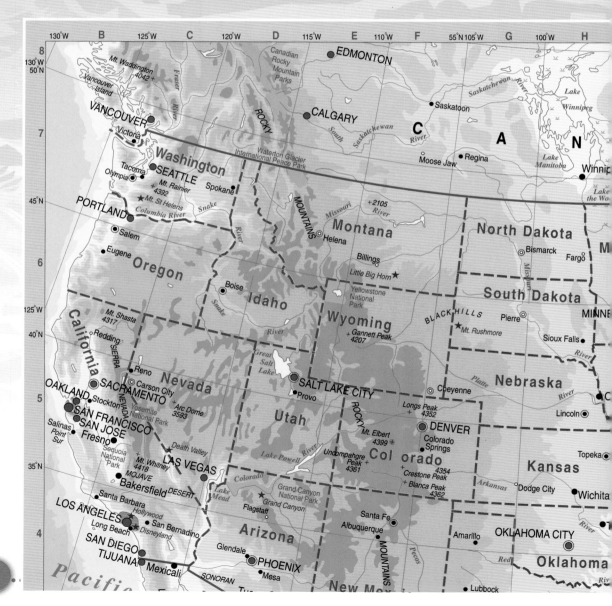

An atlas also has an index. The index lists the places named on the maps. Atlas indexes are very useful. They list the map number and the grid coordinates of places. This helps you find these places in the atlas.

Place Name	Map Number	Grid Coordinate
Atlanta	94	K4
Atlantic City	94	M5
Atlantic Ocean	61	N5
Auckland	67	F6

LET'S EXPLORE MATH

Look at the map of the United States of America. List all the cities found in the cells at these grid coordinates.

a. E6

b. H5

c. G6

d. Explain what you did to find these cities.

Symbols and Keys

Maps use **symbols** (SIM-buhls) to show things. Symbols are pictures that stand for something else. Buildings might be black squares. A forest might be a green area. A road might be a gray line. The meaning of the symbols is shown in a **key**.

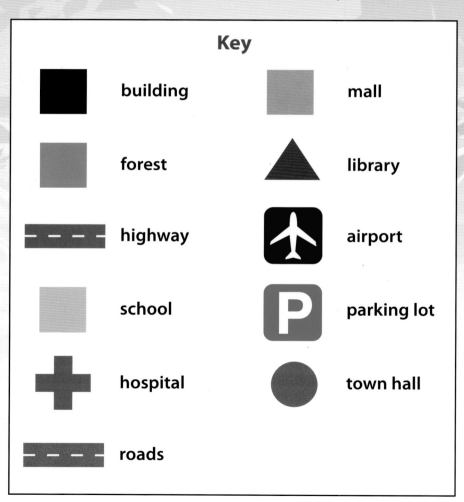

Key

building

forest

highway

school

hospital

roads

mall

library

airport

parking lot

town hall

Now look at this city map. Look at the symbols in the key. Can you find all the symbols on the map?

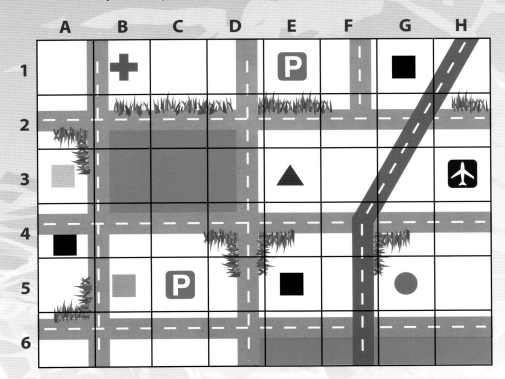

LET'S EXPLORE MATH

Use the key on page 10 and the street map above to answer the questions below.

Write the grid coordinates for:

a. the school.   **b.** the hospital.   **c.** the library.

What city features would you find at these coordinates?

d. E1   **e.** H3   **f.** B5

Symbols vary on different maps. This map of the 48 states shows the states and some capital cities. Capital cities are shown with stars. How are the other cities shown on the map? How are the borders of the states shown on the map?

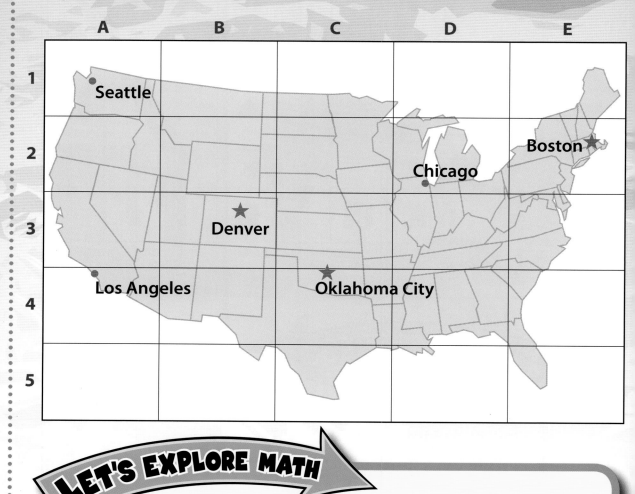

Use the map to figure out the grid coordinates for each city.

a. Los Angeles   **c.** Chicago   **e.** Denver

b. Oklahoma City   **d.** Boston   **f.** Seattle

What Is That Feature?

In some map keys, symbols look like the features that they stand for. For example, a small airplane can stand for an airport. But in other keys, symbols look nothing like what they stand for. Often, a circle on a map stands for a city.

▼ Some maps have many symbols. What do you think the anchor stands for? What do you think the plate, knife, and fork might mean?

Scale

Maps are much smaller than the areas they show. So maps have scales. Scales show how distances on a map relate to real distances. For example, 1 inch on a map might equal 50 feet on the land. So the map's scale is shown as 1 inch = 50 feet.

Scale

1 inch = 50 feet

Map Ratios

Sometimes, a map's scale is written as a **ratio**. The ratio shows one length **compared** to another length. On this map of Hawaii, the scale is a ratio. It is written like this: 1:7,000,000 cm. This ratio means that 1 centimeter on this map stands for 7 million centimeters in real life. That is 70 kilometers.

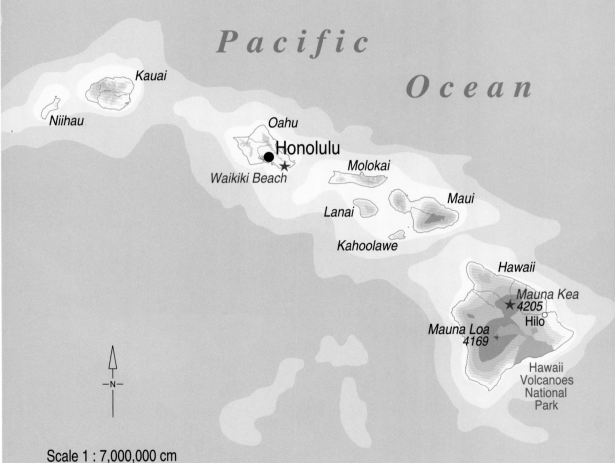

Pacific

Ocean

Kauai

Niihau

Oahu

Honolulu

Waikiki Beach

Molokai

Maui

Lanai

Kahoolawe

Hawaii

Mauna Kea
★4205
Hilo

Mauna Loa
4169 +

Hawaii
Volcanoes
National
Park

—N—

Scale 1 : 7,000,000 cm

Working Out Distance

A map can show the distance between two points. A map's scale helps us work out this distance. This information can be really useful. How far do you need to travel to get somewhere? A map can give you the answer.

Reading a Map

Many maps have grid coordinates, a key, and a scale. You can use these maps to find both location and distance.

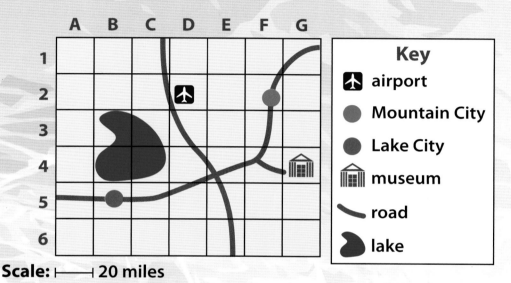

Scale: ├──┤ 20 miles

LET'S EXPLORE MATH

Use the key and the scale to answer the questions below. If you are driving, about how many miles are there between:

a. Mountain City and Lake City?

b. the airport and Mountain City?

c. the airport and the museum?

Compasses

Compasses show **direction** (duh-REK-shuhn). Compasses have at least four points. These points are: north, south, east, and west. Each point can be measured in degrees. North is where we start at 0°. East is at 90° and south is at 180°. West is located at 270°. The whole way around the compass is 360°.

Map Compasses

On a map, a compass rose always points north. This helps you figure out directions on a map.

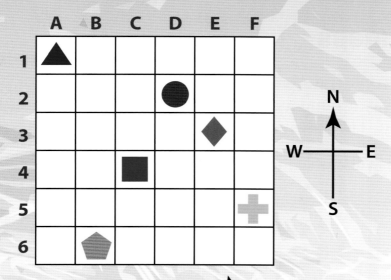

LET'S EXPLORE MATH

Use the compass rose to answer these questions. Write the grid coordinates for each answer.

a. Which shape is north of D5?

b. Which shape is west of F1?

c. Which shape is east of C5?

d. Which shape is south of B1?

e. Which shape is north of E6?

f. Which shape is east of B4?

Different Maps

Maps can be made for different purposes.

Street Maps

Many people use street maps. Street maps help people find their way around a city or town. The streets are named on the maps. The maps may also show other features.

▼ A street map of Washington, D.C.

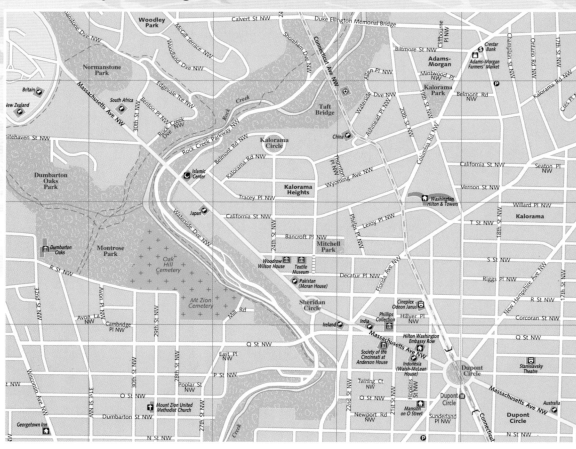

Tourist Maps

Some maps only show features such as walking trails, mountains, and lakes. Hikers use maps like these. The maps show the places they want to visit. Which places would you visit on this map?

▼ Tourist map of the Kīlauea area of the Hawaii Volcanoes National Park

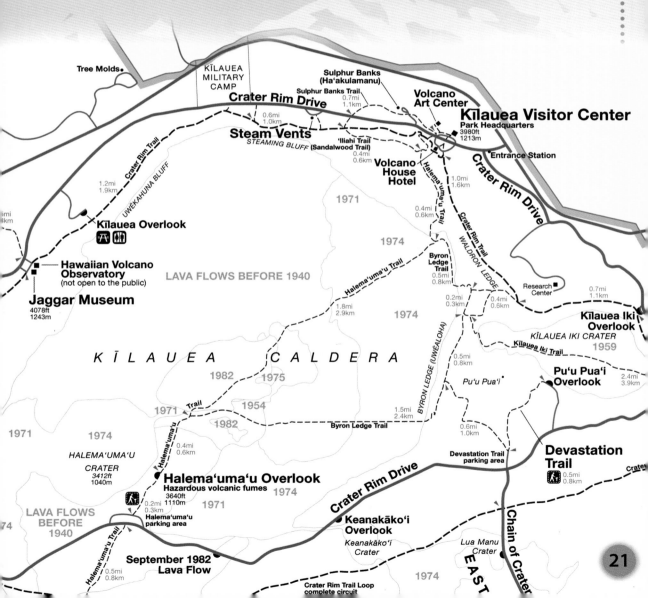

Tree Molds

KĪLAUEA MILITARY CAMP

Sulphur Banks (Ha'akulamanu)

Crater Rim Drive

Sulphur Banks Trail
0.7mi
1.1km

Volcano Art Center

Kīlauea Visitor Center
Park Headquarters

0.6mi
1.0km

Steam Vents
STEAMING BLUFF (Sandalwood Trail)

'Iliahi Trail
0.4mi
0.6km

3980ft
1213m

Entrance Station

Crater Rim Drive

1.2mi
1.9km

UWĒKAHUNA BLUFF

Volcano House Hotel

1971

1.0mi
1.6km

Kīlauea Overlook

0.4mi
0.6km

Hawaiian Volcano Observatory
(not open to the public)

1974

Byron Ledge Trail
0.5mi
0.8km

Crater Rim Trail

Research Center

0.7mi
1.1km

Jaggar Museum
4078ft
1243m

LAVA FLOWS BEFORE 1940

0.2mi
0.3km

0.4mi
0.6km

Kīlauea Iki Overlook

Halema'uma'u Trail

1.8mi
2.9km

1974

WALDRON LEDGE

KĪLAUEA IKI CRATER
1959

Kīlauea Iki Trail

K Ī L A U E A   C A L D E R A

1982   1975

1971   Trail

1954

1982

Byron Ledge Trail

0.5mi
0.8km

BYRON LEDGE (UWĒALOHA)

Pu'u Pua'i

Pu'u Pua'i Overlook

2.4mi
3.9km

1.5mi
2.4km

1971

1974

1971

HALEMA'UMA'U CRATER
3412ft
1040m

0.4mi
0.6km

Halema'uma'u Trail

0.6mi
1.0km

Devastation Trail parking area

Devastation Trail
0.5mi
0.8km

Crater

Halema'uma'u Overlook
Hazardous volcanic fumes
3640ft
1110m

1974

Crater Rim Drive

0.2mi
0.3km

Halema'uma'u parking area

1971

LAVA FLOWS BEFORE 1940

74

September 1982 Lava Flow

Halema'uma'u Trail

0.5mi
0.8km

Keanakāko'i Overlook

Keanakāko'i Crater

Lua Manu Crater

Chain of Crater

EAST

Crater Rim Trail Loop
complete circuit

1974

Population Map

This is a population map of China. Darker colors show where more people live. You need to use the key to find out what the different colors show. Where do most people live in China?

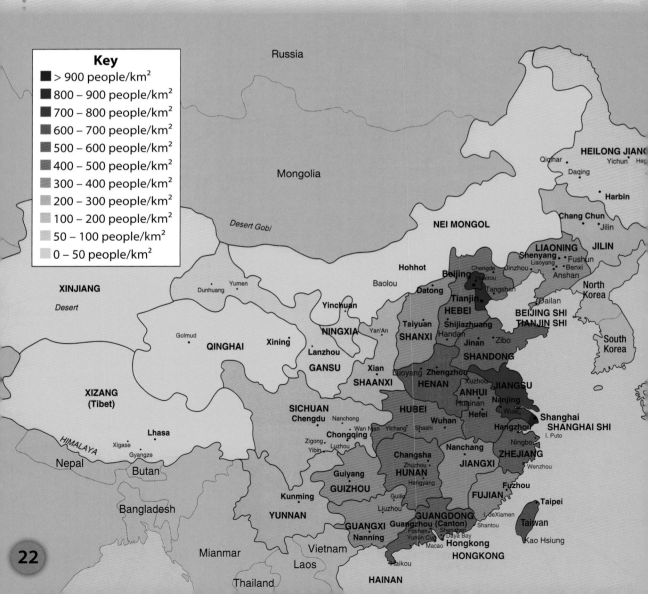

Key
- > 900 people/km²
- 800 – 900 people/km²
- 700 – 800 people/km²
- 600 – 700 people/km²
- 500 – 600 people/km²
- 400 – 500 people/km²
- 300 – 400 people/km²
- 200 – 300 people/km²
- 100 – 200 people/km²
- 50 – 100 people/km²
- 0 – 50 people/km²

Russia

Mongolia

Desert Gobi

NEI MONGOL

HEILONG JIANG
Qiqhar • • Yichun • Heg
• Daqing

• Harbin

Chang Chun •
• Jilin

LIAONING   JILIN
Shenyang • • Fushun
Liaoyang • • Benxi
Jinzhou • • Anshan

XINJIANG

Desert

Dunhuang •   Yumen •

Hohhot •

Chengde •
Beijing • Huairou •
Baolou   • Tangshan
Datong • Tianjin •
HEBEI
Shijiazhuang •
Taiyuan • Handan •
SHANXI   • Jinan • Zibo
Yan'An •   SHANDONG

Golmud •

QINGHAI   Xining •

Yinchuan •

NINGXIA

Lanzhou •

GANSU   Xian •
Xian •

SHAANXI

Luoyang • Zhengzhou •
HENAN

• Dailan

BEIJING SHI
TIANJIN SHI

North
Korea

South
Korea

XIZANG
(Tibet)

SICHUAN
Chengdu • Nanchong •

Lhasa •
Xigase •
Gyangze •

Nepal   Butan

HIMALAYA

Chongqing •
Wan Nian Yichang •
Zigong • Yibin Luzhou •

Bangladesh

Kunming •
YUNNAN

Xuzhou •
ANHUI   Nanjing •
Huainan •   JIANGSU
Hefei •   • Wuxi
HUBEI   Shanghai
Wuhan •   Hangzhou • SHANGHAI SHI
• I. Puto
Shashi •   • Ningbo
ZHEJIANG
Nanchang •   • Wenzhou
Changsha • JIANGXI
Zhuzhou •
HUNAN
Hengyang •   Fuzhou •
Guiyang •   • Taipei
GUIZHOU   Guilin •   FUJIAN
Liuzhou •   Kao Hsiung
GUANGDONG   • deXiamen
GUANGXI Guangzhou (Canton) • Shantou
Nanning • Foshan • • Shenzhen   Taiwan
Yunfu Cun • Daya Bay
Macao • Hongkong
• Haikou   HONGKONG

Mianmar   Vietnam
Laos
Thailand   HAINAN

Land-Use Map

The map below shows how the land is used for farming in Australia. The map shows what kind of land uses there are and where they are.

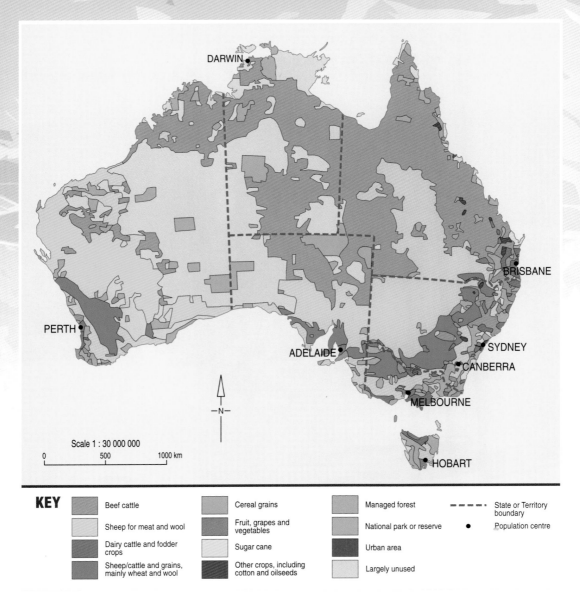

DARWIN

PERTH

ADELAIDE

MELBOURNE

BRISBANE

SYDNEY

CANBERRA

HOBART

↑
—N—

Scale 1 : 30 000 000

0   500   1000 km

KEY

	Beef cattle
	Sheep for meat and wool
	Dairy cattle and fodder crops
	Sheep/cattle and grains, mainly wheat and wool
	Cereal grains
	Fruit, grapes and vegetables
	Sugar cane
	Other crops, including cotton and oilseeds
	Managed forest
	National park or reserve
	Urban area
	Largely unused

– – – – State or Territory boundary

• Population centre

Making Maps

A person who makes maps is called a **cartographer** (car-TOG-ruh-fer). Long ago, cartographers used to draw maps by hand. Before printing was invented, copies of maps were also made by hand. Today, cartographers use computers to help them make maps.

▼ A cartographer at work

Working with Maps

Do you like drawing and working on computers? Are you interested in the environment and in science? And do you enjoy doing mathematics? If so, then perhaps you might like to work with maps.

Land surveyors (ser-VAY-uhrz) use maps. So do truck drivers and pilots. Astronomers use maps, too. But they use maps of the sky, not the land!

A land surveyor at work ▼

Changing Maps

Maps change as information about our world changes. A map of the world did not show the Americas until 1507.

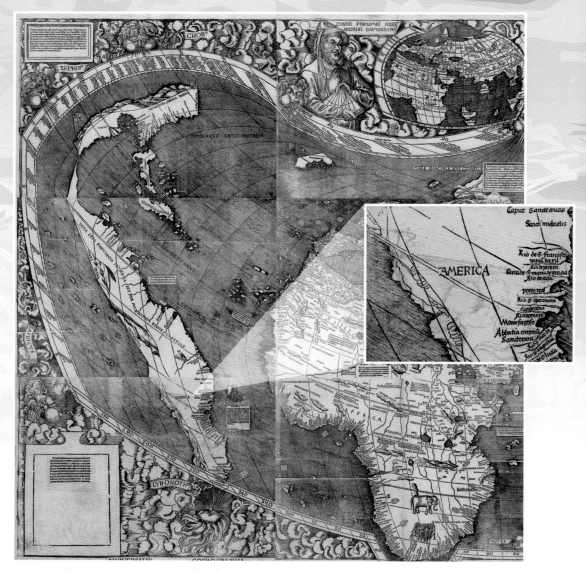

▲ This famous map was the first map to use the name "America."

Maps Are Everywhere

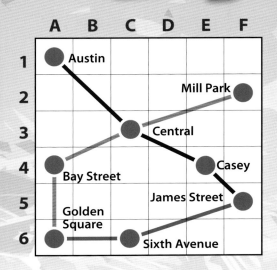

Maps really are everywhere. Think about your neighborhood. Your local subway has a map showing all the stations. Your local park may have a map showing walking trails. You probably see and use maps every day. You'll never get lost again!

LET'S EXPLORE MATH

Use the subway map above to answer these questions.

a. Write the grid coordinates for each station.

b. If you got on the subway at James Street and went to Mill Park, what stations would you pass through?

c. Explain why there may be more than one correct answer for b.

Getting Home

This is a street map of Sierra's town. Today, Sierra will visit each location on her way home from school. First, she has to run some errands for her mom. She also wants to meet her friends at the playground. Last, Sierra has a swimming lesson.

The map of Sierra's town is shown below on a coordinate plane. A coordinate plane is a lot like a grid map. It has labels, horizontal and vertical lines, and sections. But coordinate planes are labeled on the lines, not the spaces. The point is labeled where 2 lines cross. Most of the time, coordinate planes use only numbers to label the lines. For example, on the map below, the library is on point (5, 6).

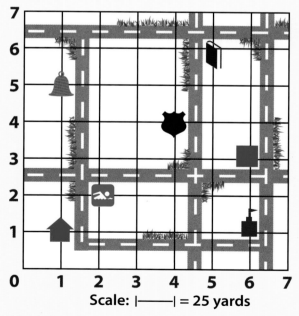

Scale: |——| = 25 yards

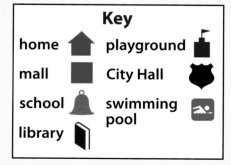

Key

home		playground	
mall		City Hall	
school		swimming pool	
library			

Solve It!

a. Write the grid coordinates and approximate compass directions for a route Sierra could take.

b. Work out the distance Sierra traveled on this route.

Use the steps below to help you explain the route you chose for Sierra.

Step 1: Plan Sierra's route. Write the grid coordinates for each location in the order in which Sierra will visit them.

Step 2: Use approximate compass directions (north, south, east, west) to describe the route Sierra took. For example, start at (1, 5) head east to (5, 5).

Step 3: Use the scale to work out approximately how far Sierra traveled.

Is There Another Way?

c. Is there a different route Sierra could take that covers a shorter distance?

Glossary

cartographer—a person who draws maps

compared—having looked at the features of two or more things

direction—the line or route in which something is moving, facing, or pointing

features—the main parts of things

forecast—to predict something will happen in the future, using information you have

image—a drawing or photograph

key—a list that explains symbols used in a map

land surveyors—people who collect, study, or inspect land measurements

latitude—horizontal lines shown running east to west on maps

locations—the points, positions, or places in which some people or some things are

longitude—vertical lines shown running north to south on maps

ratio—a comparison of two quantities; one amount is a fraction of the other

symbols—letters or simple pictures that have widely recognized meanings

Index

Let's Explore Math

Page 6:
a. C2　**b.** D2　**c.** D3　**d.** D4　**e.** A2　**f.** C5

Page 9:
a. Salt Lake City, Provo
b. Oklahoma City, Tulsa, Wichita, Topeka
c. Cheyenne, Pierre
d. Answers will vary.

Page 11:
a. A3　**b.** B1　**c.** E3　**d.** the parking lot　**e.** the airport　**f.** the mall

Page 12:
a. A4　**b.** C4　**c.** D2　**d.** E2　**e.** B3　**f.** A1

Page 17:
a. About 120 miles　**b.** About 110 miles　**c.** About 80 miles

Page 19:
a. circle　**b.** triangle　**c.** cross　**d.** pentagon　**e.** diamond　**f.** square

Page 27:
a. Austin – A1; Mill Park – F2; Central – C3; Bay Street – A4; Casey - E4; James Street – F5; Golden Square – A6; Sixth Avenue – C6.
b. Casey and Central OR Sixth Avenue, Golden Square, Bay Street, and Central.
c. Answers will vary.

Problem-Solving Activity

a. Answers will vary but should include grid coordinates and compass directions.
b. Answers will vary depending on the route chosen.

Sample Route

Step 1: School: (1, 5); Library: (5, 6); City Hall: (4, 4); Mall: (6, 3); Playground: (6, 1); Swimming: (2, 2); Home: (1, 1).

Step 2: (1, 5) head east to (5, 5). Head north to (5, 6). Then head south to (5, 4). Go west to (4, 4). Then go south to (4, 3). Head east to (6, 3). Head south to (6, 1). Then head west to (2, 1). Head north to (2, 2). Head west to (1, 2). Then head south to (1, 1).

Step 3: (1, 5) head east to (5, 5) = 100 yards. Head north to (5, 6) = 25 yards.
So school to library = 125 yards.
(5, 6) head south to (5, 4) = 50 yards. Head west to (4, 4) = 25 yards.
So library to city hall = 75 yards.
(4, 4) go south to (4, 3) = 25 yards. Head east to (6, 3) = 50 yards.
So city hall to mall = 75 yards.
(6, 3) head south to (6, 1) = 50 yards.
So mall to playground = 50 yards.
(6, 1) head west to (2, 1) = 100 yards. Head north to (2,2) = 25 yards.
So playground to swimming pool = 125 yards.
(2, 2) head west to (1, 2) and south to (1, 1) = 50 yards.
So swimming pool to home = 50 yards.

125 yards + 75 yards + 75 yards + 50 yards + 125 yards + 50 yards = 500 yards. Sierra traveled 500 yards.

c. Answers will vary.